RUNNING OUT OF ENGLAND

Will Daunt

Will Daunt.

Oversteps Books

Text and photographs byWill Daunt

ISBN 0 954137663

First published 2004 by
Oversteps Books
Froude Road
Salcombe
South Devon TQ8 8LH

Oversteps Books acknowledges
the financial assistance of
Arts Council England South West

Printed in Great Britain by The Printing Press
21 Clare Place
Coxside
Plymouth PL4 0JW

ALSO BY WILL DAUNT

Lancashire Working (K.T. Publications, 2003)
Houses Dim & 2000 Tales of Love Rewinding
(Grendon House, 2000 & 2001)

ACKNOWLEDGEMENTS include

FIRST TIME, PENNINE PLATFORM, THE THIRD HALF, SEPIA, ENVOI, VOICES, POETRY NOW NORTH WEST 1997, THE POETRY CHURCH, THE EAGLE & THE LION, POET'S ENGLAND: LANCASHIRE, AMMONITE, POETRY NOW (NORTHERN ENGLAND 2001 & 2002), C.P.R., POET IN THE ROUND, THE GREEN BOOK, PERIOD PIECE AND PAPERBACK, PURPLE PATCH, SMOKE, NEON HIGHWAY, LIVING POETS and LINKS

'Running Out of England' features uncollected poems, as well as those from two collections published by the now defunct Grendon House.

FROM REVIEWS

The poems create a great atmosphere and bring to life the tiny, perilous villages, the dramatic scenery and the sense of living on the edge of existence. The use of imagery is excellent.
SEPIA

Strange ways of life are presented as normality ... It's an excellent though disturbing collection.
N.H.I. REVIEW

... set to a diary of dates; tales of travel and stillness, from forgotten names to millennium eve in the poet's deadpan but clever language.
The Affectionate Punch

Will is very good at creating a bleakness which at times can be chilly but is never damp and scary. Read it and be over the hills and far away. Pleasing.
Krax

This collection of poems could well have been called A Book of Forms such is the scope and craftsmanship of Will Daunt's work. This collection is ultimately worth the graft of the reader. Will Daunt is building a fine body of work, one that warrants a more comprehensive collection sooner rather than later.
John G. Hall, N.H.I. REVIEW

Deals with place and time, sometimes writes eloquently and at other times, raw and straight to the point. Interesting use of language of imagery. I enjoyed this collection.
Alice Lenkiewicz, in NEON HIGHWAY 8

... the narrator of Lancashire Working is a fascinated outsider, reflecting on a landscape and community he feels an affinity towards but whose history and culture continue to tease and exclude him. The stance is removed rather than remote, reflective and analytical not judgemental.
Bob Mee in IOTA 63

Beneath the surface of Daunt's poems there are the constant reminders of the changes which have taken place. Lancashire, as the cover photographs show, is no longer a grim industrial landscape, but an area of mixed affluence ... Daunt takes the familiar, even banal details of life and uses indirect imagery to present an original interpretation.
Ingrid Riley in PULSAR 36

CONTENTS

RUNNING OUT OF ENGLAND

Will Daunt

For Mum and Dad

LEAVING EXMOOR

Coming meant just
the postponement of summer,
apples still tiny,
great grass in far orchards.

Leaving, we heard
how the torrents erupted,
stifling the foxgloves
in waterlogged boltholes.

Leaving was deep
as if mummified, where
in the bog-sponge
our fossils lay trodden.

Leaving looked sodden,
with tracks and the batteries
choking in throbs
as the walls dived away.

Leaving was grey
with the lambless to cling to,
nests in the river
and branches ripped early.

Leaving was nearly
the last fall, that battered wheat
strung to the earth
- while machineries rusted.

CUMBRIAN JUNCTIONS

Spring 2001

A car which threw the group who drove
against the swell of trippers, south,
recorded, in a glaze, the land
of bright and focused genocide.

The grazing, almost-shone and short
in April, fresh as ash, vacated
like a drift, flopped off the cusp
of furnaces by hillside homes.

All vehicles vented up the reek
of holocaust, de-sensitised
on oil-painted, fuming scarp
on spring-crime, where the water washed.

Like surgeons' gloves, escaping clean
all drove to shield their globular
and seed-fed lives, domains, calf-razed
and foot-in-mouth, but soon retrieved.

HULL,

2 December 1985

By a wharf that sand is sucking,
After days in rankled sidings,
In the trolleys, drowned for ages,
Under an arch across the barges,
Over a Head half-spurned
And fog horns,

'there is an evening coming in'.

Out of a pen, eked in the last place
From each booth, too rank for carping,
Out of a frown at the terminus
Goes
                    'one never seen before,
that lights no lamps'.

1979

Showers were toppling the angular clump,
old walls over contours, those breaches
and arms throughout Shropshire.

They rolled in like assonance, shading
alliterative dusks and the ditches
that winter had slurried.

You were there, trying to stand
with a faltering drift underfoot
like the thickness of word.

Sentences trailed beyond Wilderhope,
melting that whiteout to fields
which emerged with the decade.

DIGITAL MEMORY

Six family prospects
shut in the picture:

lad, with a pained eye
filming the thigh of the land. Action!

Vying for vantage, girls
view-find the landshape. Snap!

Granddad tilts gawps
at a scree-side of chances. Taken …

Mum's on the edge,
out of focus, remotely posed,

and Dad's panning polythene worlds
he can upload at home, or shoot off as mail

LESSON IN LONELINESS

Salisbury Plain

Imagining Imber, we remember
roads unstringing
half the Plain, wheeling orderlies
each September to vacant beds.

Autumn there, unstaunched and hungry
croons a warning,
like the shelling of an arc
that holes a crater. Something balked

from plough to padlock;
here's the chart of a stricken ward,
its walls collapsing.
Summer shakes up American Road

ricocheting with prose, rebuilt, redrafted.
Those who need the work, engrave it
like a pillbox, for their teachers.
There they wait, our younger Imbers.

LENT-in-MENDIP

Here's a butt for weeks on end,
where the barrows weave a sackcloth.

They are leaden flues, like carbines
emptying their ore around us.

Roofs are kneeling in the tinder,
burning from inside, the trauma.

Trees that stand, like buttresses
hide the homeless weeks on end.

Wilder still, a stranded trig point
spans the aimless growth, the slag pits.

All recalls more glowing flora
and the weeks on end, the trauma.

NOT GIOTTO

Cometprobe, 1986

Beams though valleys
have threaded us here
while night grew;

bruised out of day-synch and silken,
probes of ours lie stitched in tight.

Meanwhile, Halley
is unzipping wildly
seventy years;

jangled, his shrapnel
flails an unpatterned world-scheme,

resetting dials. Watchers
curse the scrapped decades -

yet we hoard days.

AUGHTON PARK

Not *Adlestrop*

Yes. Some remembered Aughton Park –
the shame of every afternoon.
That view which trees reduced to,
unassumingly, autumn to June.

The rails groaned. Kids called or jeered.
Or left for a home that paid
up steps, in uniforms. All they knew
was Aughton, grander than a park -

and broad-leaved, broadening, grassy
and overshown, with stock-paved drives -
no steel-grey or blowing hard
of gritty spirals in the sky.

And for their childhoods a blackbird sang
close by. Down the line, resounded
further and darker, jackdaw calls
from Merseyside and Lancashire.

MOTORWAY

The new river drains a city,
sliproads suck the pasture.
Blackness.

Like a spillage, the new traffic
buries time, to roar
at midnight.

No-one wonders at the flux of dead air
on a verge to nowhere,
rusting sideways.

Stuffed with flotsam, the new speeds
vent many senseless -
grass ungrazed,

no muck-spread comfort, in the new-stained
clapped-out fear
of tarmac shadow,

printed to death. Day renews the black meanders
on white lines.
Limbs dissolve.

WHITE SETTLERS

West Lancashire

A white farm in a kink of land
is the tabletful of what we hope

and where a planed-out charm injects,
from the level Moss, sliding under rain.

An unmade road, like a teenage arm,
cradles everywhere we never drive,

the wall of calm by the sepia field
looks bleached, like home, with the mortgage paid.

That hooked-on harm of twenty-five years
is a punctured sleep where the sky lies down,

where name and number are well alarmed,
and spike what we'd like with who we are,

like a dream of farms. Think of a trip,
recall where the memories cannot start,

and you're here, lying. Sweat runs, from palm to palm
pushing land and youth and home apart.

HALFWAY

Clamber up the railway ridge
and see, at half your final age,
the rungs which trod a life of scrub

and wonder when the best (and worst)
pulled out. It's linear
and poorly used, this landscape,

half of seventy years,
a flopped out, filleted
lying down. Hackneyed axes

of pen, paper, line, land,
seize up at the station space

in stationary ageing.

THE UPSIDE TOWN

1/1/96

from the Beacon's brow
was a galaxy of lights below.

As dusk elapsed on New Year's Day,
the apertures and time delays
could not expand or give the lie
to that grey template of the sky.

The new town, lit up, slid indoors,
like a star-flung sea, on broken shores.

WHERE HE FELL

The Captain's House

His yellow house leaves rope enough
to hinge upon.
Its door swings like cartilage
on dusted bone.

His children's kids touch up and scrape
the plastering;
a last emulsion hangs, like home,
without, within.

The firebeds, his flowerplace
may glow again,
but only as an ageing post
for younger men.

Hints of where his colour held
forever fade,
and decades fall to penetrate
a mustard shade.

OCTOBER

or

hating the choice of love or work
that lives in a life of noughts,

as if

2000 geese would choose
between some amnesty on Earth,

or fly

to cast off fields that bleach below
our sown initials in the sky.

A LANCASHIRE GLEN

Summer's an odd clough, as dark as they numb,
or a peel of blue
wrung from sponge-slopes. Cold heaven.

Summer's the stone path, pebbled to mulch point
or inside a lee
of forgotten fields, buried here.

Summer's those hogweed, cut loose in the dogmire
and waving aloft
like a standard, that routed earth.

Summer's the moss, flaking out of a sand-side
and every lit icon
of somewhere undrowned, or its sound

in this summer-shorn niche out of water.
I hear where it hurls
as it widens for winter, the same grid

and ground,
unfound by the map-gang.

CARRION

While petted life, in its metal room
hardened out of then,
they buried a couple of lies

and sent all to bed. By the dying place,
where a chill-gripped
darkness awoke irreversibly,

none stirred at the stroke
of mid-nought, to hear
an ether-wound metronome.

The hide froze and tongue aged
as mouths became ageless,
and auras of zero awaited

the sun. When a firstfall
trod dawnstairs, down
to the jamb, Dad, Mum, numb,

knocked on the vortex
of breathlessness now.
Old friends of every day

heard, in a lauded-void,
'*This is the first fear*
you hoard, going Godless.'

DAWN CARNAGE

Paint on the phone booth,
a blood-stuck scene, too brightly
shades an exhaled clot.

Another second,
and a life, its pall of breath
will remain unzipped.

Eighteen well-sealed years
of racing the unbought car,
has been slid aside.

That whining prospect
veering nowhere, sits astride
the layby, spent-up.

Well within ear-shock,
two blood-letting cathode homes
flicker, vortexical.

B 5240

Winter

2 kilometres

of tar scraping bare,
and faith paused on path-scars,   then

800 metres

recorded by lamps
after hope, head-to-dark.   Soon,

10 cat’s eyes left,

of that fast-winding
tract to work, done

at the junction,

and seconds from home,
like playing back heaven,

the 2000 spool.

MILESTONE ON DARK LANE

December 1999

While each of the minutes in all of our lives
is speeding away where the decade survives,
Your way holds true.

Where arched rhododendron replaces the sky,
the last local metres are measured in stone
that no-one made new.

Like signwriters stuck for millennial verse
or slogans to boast what we shall be, or were,
we erect words to You,

these square, two dimensional
tokens and static tracks, framing
our faith like a view.

How easy to wear out the verge
in nostalgia, for what we might pray
the big moment could do.

Yet, now in the scars of the road
and its finite kerbs, we could wind up
without end, without learning

to try again here, not revolt, but renew.

WINTER CROP

2001

Out of farm's way
tractors grabbed that August
stalking walls.

Any home

got sown with tracers,
metaphors rolled
the drumming mind.

September

grew unmeasured
news. More fodder surged
and, in the chill,

a slice of Britain

greened, as if with troops
on littered drill yards. Earth threw
out our future food

and mines like these.

GREENING GROUND ZERO

However fast the dust drains night from day,
wherever silence clogs your urban pores,
whenever you evoke that yesterday,
whoever grieves, remember,

more new shores

roll out beyond the rubble -

U.S.A.

ORMSKIRK BORDERS

And on a rise
of roots and moss,
the quarry ends,
well overrun.

A sandstone town
was unearthed here,
its paths disperse
towards elsewhere.

Some underpin
an upland arc,
where fields succeed
or towns might be,

and others merge
where railways died,
on mounds that lie
like boundaries.

Behind all this
goes Lancashire.
The farms run down
the walls are wide,

and where it lay
it ends, and there
where sunsets rise
the city flares.

MONDAYS

are moments
in scrubby meadows,
where mists tinge the root
with something
tubercular;

are inaudible throes
you miss breathless,
where dusk
is the bleeding throat
wheezing infections;

are the whispers
you cannot hear
soaking the deep combes;

is the moor
you're allowing
to ooze through your mind.

FRIENDS REUNITE

across the platforms.
Luggage stretches, shadows loom.
Time gleams, deserted.

Opposite sides of metal, cleft
or youth stuck deep in the ether:

hope … and hope … and hype.

Suppose we've been there too:
should someone let the trains
tear through, perhaps on time

like life (and other sites
where we and lesser pasts of us belong)?

SELF-ERASER

Odd, what he could write or say,
twenty years before today,
and the fact that no-one knew
progress locked, rejections grew.

Many negatives of change
did nothing to extend his range.
But now computers help the man
to boast that one who could not, can.

YOU BUY A LIFE TO LAST

and see
how large it stands,
how solidly.

The frame of where to live
is sure,
the sides remote,
a room, no door.

And growing into space
you know
not when to spread,
nor how to slow,

until the box's lid
is prised,
upon the stroke
of being wise,

then you, like someone less,
will be
the pleasured mess
on what's outside,

not dispossessed
of any shape,
what was immersed
won't unescape.

BEDROOM PICTURE

Under Klimt
there has to be
a new, or personal
tapestry

of words, and
clasping certainties
you will not need
to light, or free,

and Love, much more
than artistry
lies here, for you,
in the dark, from me.

LOST ONE

1. Weeks From Safety

You had been weeks
in the blizzard,
where your freeze-frame
left us, parents
on the scanner,
people, warmer
near your icy,
drifted portrait.
Two dimensions
screened your body,
while the widened
world was noisy,
shaking sonar
through the fissures.
Life, the abyss,
half-filled itself.
Your measured head
was buoyant, broad,
your bound-up limbs
were inches long.

2. A Colder Birth

A clattering
of beds, befores
and afters, last
minutes living,
took him beyond
becoming old.
We rolled away
from chatter, down
maternity's
embankment. Strange,
the simple words
miscarried there;
there, as comfort
strung together.
Then the scuttled
disconnecting:
life, like a plug,
tugged out, sucked in,
and hanging down
and helpless, there.

3. Disconnecting

That night, I drove
whole cranes away,
ultimate hopes
swung over him,
his closure in
a colder birth.
That year soon lost
the Christmas trees,
wards were to fall
and leave our life
rebuilt on his.
The hospital
had nought to show
but scaffolding,
nothing beyond
the empty branch.
Winter zigzags
brought him outdoors,
no cold, no warmth,
from end to end.

4. In The Blizzard

I mind about
a tongue, made up
to be soundless,
it's imprinted
weeks from safety
like a memory.
What reminds us
how to speak it
is the brother
not receiving.
Without language,
he found sleeping,
spoke the silent
undertone. Here
another sleeps
but sideways, lost
to brotherhood
and early words,
too quiet yet
for sounding out.

2000 POEMS

15 January

Write as much as you like of that sad, romantic stuff,
but for all their tears, the lovers have had enough.
They're making a stand at the end of every phone,
and pleading that they can be left, bereft, alone.

The internet geeks are pleading for love off-line
while colleges tip out their poets, studying crime.
My library's remaindered a last vestige of verse,
and schools have outlawed sonnets, odes, and worse.

It's trendy to lose the comfort of knowing why
seasons and landscapes have turned the writer shy.
There's no one I know with a mortgage and time to say
how their love is imbued with colours of yesterday.

But through the chill of the next two thousand years,
she melts my heart, as I hope she knows, or hears.

Burns' Night

They drove me away to be part of a team
at the dark hotel, where juggernauts crawl.
And I squeezed my life in a case for the day
but unpacked what it meant on my own that night.

By dinner our food chain had half-emerged
from armchairs where suits and egos purred.
The river that tickled the buildings' rim
rolled invisibly one way, back, and on.

At dawn more rain assailed each room,
waking a weekend. The Ribble raged.
By degrees, we managed to slip away
like remnants of what had been once, recalled,

and I lost any sense of rhyme up there,
but didn't care. You were here, composed.

14 February

I knock at the door marked 'Outstanding Career',
and lean for a while on a notice, bored.
It seems wrong to wait, right to enter, and steal
between stacks where the secrets of power are stored.

But then I look back, sunshine spot-lights the floor,
as it runs past the portraits of drab, vain and tall.
They hang like directions, but far more askew
pointing out somewhere else. Anybody would stall.

When you think of it, who have I worked for, for years?
My office is empty as tundra (and cold)
and my hard drive is cluttered with micro-debris.
The best that I've taught is what someone else sold.

Careering to nowhere I turn round and find,
love for you everywhere, one of a kind.

WHO LOST THE LOVE FILE?

29 February

'Hallo, come in. I've forgotten your name.
No don't tell me now, it is somewhere on screen,
with your details and ... oh dear, what a shame
I've deleted the life where your folder had been.

'You registered late, I attempted to fit
any profile which proved you were out of my hands.
Our recycle bin is preparing to split
with thousands like you no one else understands.

'There might be a space I could turn into yours,
in stacks or the card files behind the alarms.
There's somewhere beyond here and through the baize doors
- here is the password, now creep out of harm.'

That's how she spoke every speck of the trip,
while one more small part of him died in the chip.

DEAD-by-FORTY

15 May

Ten years back and he'd have been
as young as the dolt who ran the ship,
but mainstays of that place were seen
as old in the race for time. He died

metaphorically every day,
and lumbered his desk with the deadlines
of pride. Last week, the stowaways
cast off his final tie. He died

with the cries of his daughters
like ballast, with thrills of a love
left at home in the shredder.
A son wrote the log: how he died

to reach some fraction of that age,
working like Dad, on a different wage.

ANOTHER DAY TO LEAVE

20 July

You could not guess that how you'd worked for years
had never chalked up lifelong lines or use.
In every way, and minute of that place
the rule, however meagre, was to please.

It seemed a solid kind of home, or life
but no one frowned when you prepared to leave.
The memories of how you'd done were banked
within the building and its in-joke bunker,

and you rose, declaring, '*Here's my final day,*
a lazy way to boast of what we do.
Forgive me all I promised to improve,
indulge me when I say I still believe.'

They stacked the room with presents, and regards,
vacated time-worn chairs, and left for cars.

DOMESHOW

15 August

The trick of time is circular and
I look back at how I hoped that
love would rise from Greenwich, more than land,

a 3-D heart while others were falling flat.
The truck we hadn't had with those
who kept the Dome encased in what
they feared was a Show of failing, rose

as tumblers secured the air in knots.

The track of time was boldly laid, for
an hour, in steel, ribbon, wire and flesh, as
an arch from the nineteen hundreds wore

smooth slopes, built on a zero. That bazazz
fills our new thousands of days with the next

epoch of love, penned in hypertext.

& you said you'd never ...

September

How since that decade, friend, you've changed
and won a stage in the place called fame.
Your show is as late and as far deranged

as your longing for lust and the rest allows.
Yet we laughed louder with twenty years
less. You were the gifted and I, pretty slow

was first to applaud when it got you to work.
There was little to learn, or to buy, or to sell
in humour back there. Fast and berserk

we aped the right on, never were wrong.
But now what I mind, being stuck way out here,
is to seem set aside. Don't you still long

not to run out of ways to rewrite your life,
or seek the despair of those you loved?

NELSON, OR NOWHERE

27 September

27 September 2000
I was told, *'The 61 north out of town,*
is your best way to find where the roads disappear.
No need for a map up that causeway of dark
you'll know you're arriving when hills hit the cloud.'

Through forty low minutes I rolled under rain
which steamed from the south under stack, into lung.
Slate roofs crumpled up to the 65's rim
as wet as the last eastern peat, newly dug.

A couple of streets from an edge, where the brick
escalates to the fold, where the wrecker balls hang,
my phone called your name. I stopped on a kerb,
to hear you cut off, floating west over plains.

An e-mail at work said the rest, *Go again.*
You won't need to plan, or to drive, or return.

The Page Cannot Be Displayed

All Souls

Her glimmer-box may soon implode,
with half-saved names from somewhere, past.
They muster in the where-was-once
that never found her through the post.

It's sad but sure that one drab day
some pair within her file of spooks,
will mail each other something grim -
a virus, or the urge to speak

where devils hide. Unplug that soul
and cut her from the modem, for
the crazy part of what she'd say

recalls the will to love, when lost.
Delete each page, like those we know
we search for, but should never see.

Advent

Will this be the body in twenty years' time,
if I keep it carefully and run it indoors?
These waxes and capsules and what I decline
keep the man upright, buy off his flaws.

Shall I think this way in a decade or two,
or work an allotment of deadlines for home?
I need all the past, to look forward with you.

Could I have this family in twenty years' time
small enough to be carried, and loud with the load?
who do not yet know the right person to be
kept away from tomorrows, the contorted roads.

Shall love feel this way in a decade or two,
close like the frost, but as utter as rain
and will time post a present of futures with you?

Christmas Dawn

No birds of any tone or hue
appeal for something fresh to stop.

Diesel murmurs out of lamp range,
taxis in, and gags, and some home
false-alarms, from rattled whine
to scream. A ring of gardens,
breathing, noiseless. Nobody out, but

pigeons. Seven-ten. Some pitch
off ledges, undercut by
frozen gulls. This lightless house,
since someone died, is dim
as windows, or a rook-eyed shadow, yet

on Your day, two blackbirds nail
the odds, within a claw, of up stretched tree.

DORDOGNE LETTERS

a)

Chainsaws gnaw that glade
at dawn, and shake a valley,
traffic rattling.

e)

Frieze of fieldfares
in the slip-stream, wheeling east
on wheat-breeze, leaving.

i)

Night refills this site
in minutes, giggling kids
its dizzy filters.

o)

Lone, almond outcrops
float above two cold canoes,
or homes of boulder.

u)

Currents under us
spun tunnels – crusted, useless,
cavernous ruins.

UNDER CANVAS

Sologne Woodland

In Scotch pine woods, where Spanish oak should sway,
one army bivouacked in ragged language.

Dark peace draped,
encamped at every allocated pitch,
a mesh of fading pennants. Night could fall.

Dubliners stopped to stir, perfectly tanned,
while Parisian friends digested rainbow junk.

Some Walloons sang
and stressed in clashing shades, few Romans shrank.
Second farewells were bid to each Berliner.

These anti-types
when cast abroad, grow closer every June,
eschewing spite, that nightmared nations.

Forests furl
anew, unflagging liveries, alive, at one

and in their buried ranks, more European.

The sun-red water matches brightening sky.

A lake reheats.
Sand slopes
stir man-sprayed murk.

One swum, scooped pool
dips down,
murk creeps, kids call.

Murk spreads, wind turns,
bobs murk,
murk swaps with rain,

then thunder-water catches lightning sky.

BRETON THIRDS

1

You, free and sockless
in surf - spun coronas,
I snapped in the shallows.

2

Noon, full of surfboards
that burrow a swell, later
ripped by the jet ski.

3

Mussels in that pan,
parted where the ruddy wine
swelled between bi-valves.

A VERANDA

1

Her cask will soon be empty
and September grey. Tonight
he took the cane chairs back
to the outhouse, counting
three cicadas in the scrubland.

Etienne's goats murmured past
almost blurred under the grove,
where every dusk she'd watched
them dwindle. They called it
'Trekking through the Midi wound.'

2

A kind of lovely scar expands
above the western pen and herds.

Tomorrow the villa survives
unshuttered. Mosquitoes
die, and he stalks the sunsets
from cellar to attic, believing
that someone's frozen summer.

The china is dusted, dressing up
winter, and a lizard sweeps
towards the mistral.

Out of a crevice, pincers clip.
Two scorpions, at the death.

Roscoff's a space where summer stops,

but absently. Shadowed anglers
hurl a catch or final cast
as far and futile as the Île de Batz.

Sad causeways point the course
like love, which never ran to smooth
this coast. Will islanders

leave Brittany on swells
over drowning pools? These walkways
plummet waterwards and ferry swathes

pour up a final froth, like autumn berthing.

DIETRICH ON THE IJSSELMEER

Connie's life has slumped, and roundly,
in the years of rubber plants.
'Mother, mother ...' it will taunt her
from the glaze and yellowed tile.

When he licked at the outside door
fingers probed her dress like triggers.
As he muttered, 'Further, further ...'
half upstairs, she wouldn't stagger.

She, the sentinel, was manned
and mothered in the marram islands.
Seeping like a dune, her limbs
left love amorphous in the Zee.

He with a splashing painter, brought
her straddled girth, its silt and current
further down the garbled sluices,
beaching the slough of another sand-bar.

'Connie, mother ...' breezes called
her memories beyond the polder.
Rollers hit her thigh at high tide,
mouthing out the tang of herring.

He's an Ijsselmeer fat barge
that hiccups home on land-flat cloud,
dumping holds of motherhood
further back than arms around her.

LOCK HOLLAND

- snuff the polder winds,
fell pelts of wheat
and mill some slumped extent of sky.

Leave Holland

- shut the cycle dyke,
dredge green canals
where barges pass dim towns, adrift.

Shun Holland

- let the sand tunes loose
concealing quays,
while islands shudder out of locks, to fog.

Miss Holland

- summer's southern run,
orange and blue
or like a secret tongue, in Breton cloud.

LOW LAND

It wasn’t off an autoroute
or cobbled in the square.
Air-conditioned Europes here
were found like unsold land.

Yet, we learnt to mouth them away
with our winded torsos
empty as boulevards.

Volume was low. Belgium wheezed,

and we grew to love that tongue,
pushing back time, like the tooth in the gum.

FROM BRUSSELS AIRPORT

You flew out while we were getting fatter.
Hard as departures, the vast tarmac
had a language. We couldn't translate
the kapel under flares, trucks that sneaked
about the maternally-bulging planes;
we missed the ads as long as cafes,
saw no visor where we looked through.

Zaventum sniggered as you taxied,
subtitled flyovers, suburbs, home.

BELGIAN JOURNEY

Returning to the poplar rows,
you straddle Flanders' dykes and farms
where seasons flood and circle Bruges
or hoist their shade like skewed tarpaulins
up the line that pegs Cologne.
You read like an unfranked letter -
flung through stations, blinking where
those market stalls are huddled.

The capital is shouting space,
where villas borrow millions
to warm up art in Horta's shell.
Meanwhile, Schaerbeek and Leuven slip
as trains mingle their languages.

Beyond the Ardennes' turning point,
do not miss each stiffening winch,
its bloated slag. Drunk without work,
that Gueze slugged late in Charleroi
has barely raised a Belga haze.

Avenues here hide unsold lives,
while contours are catching themselves
beside the Semois. At Bouillon
there's game enough to forget
how forests wound the railway up.
They swallow trout and tether boar
they're lost as limestone fissures dripping
the currency of the nation.

That Belgian dash tried England too -
like something pulled from the wardrobe -
tried without fashion,
found in another land that's clashing.

AFTER ENSOR

Where the sea gave up
are casinos at dawn
and greasy promenades.
Frituurs and Maes feed the Ostendais.

The salt-swung lamps
which the sea rusts up
are half-drawn chains,
following tides down the sands' remains.

Where barnacles rise
they strip the pier head,
rinsing through the sea.

The empty quays are flat as canvas,
like a Belgian gallery
unpalletted and ending here.

LOSING WALLONIA

Always, the billowing hills
were last to be found.
Their springs fell around
dereliction of mills.

Always, the unrisen breeze
would blend with an avenue,
warping the trees
on an under-viewed land.

Always, the weather would win,
with everything damp
or as untouched as dusk.

Now, every hidden Belgian end
is warping, under-used.

CHESTNUT CITY

Chatagniers meant parallels
countlessly shelling the chaussees.
Blow upon blow of the seasoned swing,
shuddered in tallies
the Walloons knew.

Kastantjeboomen meant tramlines
cracked and hung, like Brabant.
Pummelled or unripe, that mine of mines
is the cannon
cocked in Flanders' groin.

LA VACHE QU' RIT

What a surprise you seemed
in that awkward, ambling way.
Yours was a nuzzled nudge
in its lost and lowing way
on my side and ordered *laan*.

You trampled the *boulevards*,
grinding the grey
with a green security.

MAYDANEK

Concentration Camp, Eastern Poland

Look - the picture of our guilt
at black-on-green Maydanek.
Toured-to-death we fear the rain
and less,
and then start running
into peace-talk,

I forget how many times.

Look, we wonder at the flat huts' scheme,
their ordered stain
over who they held: blue clouds
over peeled white paint - gas skies
on no man's land.
Granulated magic

I forget how many times.

Look at the random slippers here,
they run to thirty thousand,
distinguished by the lines of sweat,
and piles of wetter times.

Westerners walk through guilt
in uncremated shoes,

so ghosts get killed,

I forget how many times.

DUNMORE EAST AND WEST

From ten, the sea concedes its litres
loaning land, for a few deposits.
Out roll the strands like carpets, joined
by pools and weed-stone, careworn twins.

How these trapped shores are prised –
where cliff-dropped families gaggle and fuse.
Their B of beaches, topples sideways
into sand-soup. Breathe again.

Illogical dogs dodge missiles
thrown by kids, knee-deep and offsprung.
Half a cove of absurd surfing
paraphernalia lies, like luggage.

Various dares on breakers flume
as girl treats boy, and in the flash
of flab and lycra, tautly seamed,
two beaches shrink and separate

and every one becomes a two, or three,
reverting as they go, up sopping slipways.

BACHELORS AT AQBAL

Courtship Festival, High Atlas

They come, unbundle, merging herds
heave up without a dog or escort.
In the musty heat of August,
each leaves to his own, disperses,

learning how to lie. It prickles
in a final inch of harvest,
which the years have chewed to ritual,
meadows thinning, chopped and heartless.

Grittily, the patriarchs
are selling chips of other cultures,
moaning underneath, and aired
by polythene. The breezes titter.

Yet, some wheedle out to barter -
rubble for each guilty Frenchmen,
summits for the heady British,
who on screes have landed gliders.

Many memorise their love songs
while the batteries are lasting.
Left to mimic, off a dance floor,
women sadly stack the hayload.

These are villages in courtship,
busy in the graze, and fly-singed.
Those who leave each Aqbal leaking
possibilities of family,

pass up shrines, ignoring
rivers choked by dross, and children.

ISLANDS BY TIDE

gain phones which bind their ringing shores
with words, unstuck or unexpected.
Polarised, like rain or sunset,
now they are never being away.

When messages land, they're elongated
as fragile planes. The subsidies
have to hold, uncrease affection
and as channels
are vaster than kelp there, meshed by weather.

Each island talks of threatened waves,
with causeways like a root, but sodden.
The contact is somewhere,
almost listening,
yet it brings queries, costs the evening.

And days become hard to recall,
like a dialect gone (but good for quoting),

or unknown skerries, stacks of peat,
an empty school, the sloshing causeway.

They have been daily washing away.

TO LOFOTEN

The islands end.
Væroy, a couple of spines,
strains alone
in the rhythmic swell
of memory.

There a man reels
on the main ridge
and scuffed slopes yawn.

Mosken looks anyone's village
and cowers,
with barbed wire gardens
and dropping ways.

Wracks and sheep
crowd the landing shell,
where showers of gulls
cry threats
of possible squall.

The telephone line
sags down on the track
to the settlement,
loaded like hardship.

Its hovels are largely
havens for unanswered calls.

BEACONS SHOW FAROE

like long, feline blinks,
as we guess at what sanctuary
some must have here.

A cloud of an island
sails slow on the current,
homes reeling us in

and, spilt large,

between bright harbours,
loitering half-dusk
got a swill.

To be there,
maps in hand,
after night's out.

HOUSES DIM

off the gravel side
where this varicose tip
records Fair Isle.

Fog shakes out coughs
over blasty wrecks to Orkney,
each is counted.

Dusk, a shrunk infection
slips in white to stripe the village.
Every metre.

Blustered with its breath,
this pulse will see another summer dim

where houses were.

ABOVE AN ICE FJORD

West Greenland

This was the death pad. We squat by;
somewhere to truss up belief like an Inuit,
follow it over like waste or a sledge dog,
down ice-sheets and slobber. That was their way.
Brittle elders judged themselves - embalmed
by the grin of winter - food for the pelt.

Others, of course, crept out of life, watching
from boulders this slithered outcrop.
Wobbling there now gives a quick blink of skull,
then barks from a bluish fox hollow the heart.
She is another who follows the hunger tracks
down to Ilulissat. Heads are a first find -

in shrouds of mosquitoes.
Here with our cameras and clumsy conjectures,
we wonder how, in the splutter of daylessness,
parent and friend excused muscle and petrified
bone at the precipice; afterwards, useless flesh
nuzzled between floes. Now, in their denim,

descendants stalk girls in estate cars,
with empty guns. Cotton-lined dole is the back-
bone that shapes any dog-hauls.
Beyond the freezers and K.G.H. export stores
carcasses lie incarcerated, toyed with
in faltering Danish by bloated hands.

These, by their newest graves grow plastic sprays,
over this grinding intestine:
the ice fjord. As every lost iceberg
escapes with a ricochet, mortuaries
of the mind unfreeze, scraped like a landscape,
cast in this plaster - a modern death mask.

MIST OVER EIGG

Enough has come to come away,
a smokescreen holds the hill.
Roofs will rust and stoves can blaze
with brambles. Sedge and heather
come like a cloud below the outcrop,
low enough to soak a living.

Nowhere to drive. The outlines of van
and trailer last, where Gaelic
marks the summit, headlands, lochs,

every signpost now awry.

Visitors largely want the way
to sands that sing. Enough have come
to flush out history:

mist over land, becoming enough.

BOARDERS FROM LUING

Over a sound, there bleed
commuters, awkward and spun
out of land by the pick axe.

They are old bodies of slate
who learn of a past
where the whirlpool sings.

Parting is peat-blunt
and hills throw a shroud.

Seamless, it dribbles
the tide race down,
a ferry of memory
for homesteads to foster.

OIGH-SGEIR

You and memory
hold their favours,
skirted by the pilot's hand.

In that tall house,
piercing fathoms,
some lit lives and used to shine.

They were honed
as blind as flares
that mend the running, riddled, surf.

RHUM BURIAL

Papadil drags us from the shoulder
past an eyeless hind, through gullies,
to a loch the English hunted
sunk and sullen, ripe to moulder.

Bullough sullied ruts at random,
wanting somewhere old, built fame
but hearths out here are cold, and soon he felt
a saddle aching. Bogs encroached

as ravens tumbled through the bolder
storm of rains. We southerners
come lattice-ward, see cenotaphs,
like trunks, where summits smoulder.

Unst: the apposite end of Shetland,
once a thundered war of gods.
At Hermaness and Saxavord
a hurling out of holms from Unst.

Unst - the one portentous thud
of undercarriage or waterline tyre.
Unst, where vowel and boundary drown
at Uyeasound or Burrafirth.

Unst - a time encroached by verge
the radar over folding plains;
unsung, as thrusts on headboards
stunned with almost mustered cries.

Other Foulas

wait beyond us -
fear or ardour,

stricken heather,
death by sliding,

the unended
skua squadron

to defy. Pulled
while straining

from the Mainland
who will make it,

in that passage
to the last quay?

The vague isles lie
adrift again,

wheeling with fools.

DEMOLISHING THE COAL PLACE

1

Poised around a summer harbour,
went the light, dividing silence.
Splintered bergs were slinking through
up Vaigat and the Gulf Stream.

We saw a docile ashiness
that rolled against moraines down there,
sculling the straggled inlets
where seals dodged a skinning.

Kayaks, hoisted to that shore,
hung safe as their posterity.

Saqqaq buzzed with hearty children
gutted halibut and dog sleighs.
K.G.H.'s dried provisions
held out credit, fed our guides

then supplied a small boat
turning back to where the coal lay.

2

Europe's food, stuffed round the outboard
steers to another mess of homes.
Windows blow through seasons here
like history, without the coal.

Paunchy volunteers, we pull up
borrowed wood and burgled compounds.
Greeting visitors and autumn,
we roll down the roof and mountain

and, at a loss for twenty days,
we unearth souvenirs.

Then the partition falls, light shuts in
the expertise, the lie
we work to end. Unleashed dogs
hang as the best hope of culprits;

like a gutted heart, the village
beats out a lone twelfth year.

RONALDSAY'S WALL

Northern Orkney

Better than maps is the awkward way,
late and unheard;
Islanders bump in and stutter through hay.

Coming this far, the perimeter
(bent in the lens)
seems to have aged; but sheep recur.

When walking here (behind the sea
and turned inland),
the dyke returns, raised listlessly.

And those alive are bred by drift-weed,
like nobbled lines
or thresholds.

Crofters working up the food
have measured out ways of how to farm,
where others scrounge;
here bleats an indistinct, oily charm,

and even the vanishing rotors of death
have endpoints
that run when rusty, or grasp for breath.

GOODBYE, ISLANDS …

Pointe du Raz

Such tourists, clustered west as these
have tottered out to see lots left -

a little rack, courageous land,
point out their final fantasies:

and so it grows. Like being young,
the islands in the background, grainy,

shade a day ambitiously,
become the missing talismans –

like unrecorded songs, whose words
could curl a twingeing sense of loss,

or poems, neither primed
nor yet without the final will to give;

like bursts of gravel prose,
unsaved before the power shuts,

or prints, which now projected
face the rock, the blurring sea.

And no one gapes inland, or stops
to long for where they live, or

mull moreover, after, how
they could dread home, one afternoon …

SOME BACKGROUNDS
(with apologies for any outdated or inaccurate information)

Livestock killed during Foot & Mouth Outbreak (2001):
Over 2,000 recorded cases with nearly 4,000,000 animals slaughtered on nearly 10,000 premises

The evacuation of Imber Village in 1943:
"We were given only six weeks to get out," (Mollie Archer Smith, the last survivor of the 161 villagers).

Lead ore mining, Charterhouse-in-Mendip:
The Romans were mining as early as 49-50 AD.

Giotto Space Probe
During the night of 13/14 March 1986, this spacecraft, made history by obtaining the first close-up pictures of a comet's black, icy nucleus.

The Ormskirk-Skelmersdale Railway Line
It remained open for Goods from Ormskirk until November 1963

Death on the Roads Between 1985 and 1995, more than 10,000 teenagers died from injury in England and Wales. About 6000 were road users.

Martin Mere, Wildfowl Reserve, Lancs:
Number of pinkfeet geese recorded in October 2003: approximately 6400

Deaths in Twin Towers Attacks
Over 2,800 dead or missing, with 157 dead on the two hijacked planes. 1721 death certificates have been issued at the request of families, in cases where remains have not been identified

Membership of Friends Reunited Website
Over 10 million

Peat cut on Lancashire Fells:
Most families inhabited small villages or settlements, depending on the land to support them. They enjoyed the privilege of gathering fuel, by cutting bracken, turf, peat or brushwood.

Size of Sologne Forest (Central France):
About 5,000 sq km (1,900 sq miles)

Length of Roscoff's pedestrian walkway into the sea:
400 metres

Quantity of land reclaimed from the Zuiderzee:
165,000 hectares

Number of deaths at Maydanek Concentration camp:
50,000

Average summer temperature: South Greenland:
8-9 degrees centigrade

Island populations:
Vaeroy, Lofoten, Norway: 800
Fair Isle: 70; Eigg: 60
Luing: 200; Oigh-Sgeir: zero
Rhum: 30; Unst: 900
Foula: 40; North Ronaldsay: 90